Norwegian Recipes
Old-time Favorites

Collected by Norma Wangsness

Edited by Ann M. Bauer, Dorothy Crum, Michelle Nagle S
Morten Strand, and Joan Liffring-Zug.

Rosemaling by Norma Wangsness

Approximate Metric Equivalents

1/4 teaspoon = 1.23 milliliters
1/2 teaspoon = 2.46 milliliters
3/4 teaspoon = 3.7 milliliters
1 teaspoon = 4.93 milliliters
1 1/4 teaspoons = 6.16 milliliters
1 1/2 teaspoons = 7.39 milliliters
1 3/4 teaspoons = 8.63 milliliters
2 teaspoons = 9.86 milliliters
1 tablespoon = 14.79 milliliters
2 tablespoons = 29.57 milliliters
1/4 cup = 59.15 milliliters

1/2 cup = 118.3 milliliters
1 cup = 236.59 milliliters
2 cups or 1 pint = 473.18 milliliters
3 cups = 709.77 milliliters
4 cups or 1 quart = 946.36 milliliters
4 quarts or 1 gallon = 3.785 liters

Temperature
To get Celsius (Centigrade) when
Fahrenheit is known: subtract 32,
multiply by 5, divide by 9.

ISBN 0-941016-43-9
Copyright Penfield Press

Contents

Norwegian Recipes:
About the Author

Norma Wangsness, volunteer for Vesterheim, the Norwegian-American Museum, preserves her Norwegian-American heritage in many ways. Her artistic skills include painting and rosemaling, in addition to the preparing of great foods. In compiling this collection, Norma selected family favorites and recipes she has used for many years. Norwegian-American cooks are noted for their use of almond and dill for delicate and flavorful seasonings. These recipes also include the old favorites of delicious cookies, light cakes, sweet breads, lefse and the traditional root vegetables.

Sites of Norwegian-American Interest

Vesterheim (Vesterheim means western home)
The Norwegian-American Museum
Decorah, Iowa
This is one of the great folk art museums of North America devoted to a single immigrant culture. Nordic Fest is held the last full weekend in July in Decorah, about one hundred fifty miles south of Minneapolis-St. Paul, Minnesota.

Little Norway
Blue Mounds, Wisconsin
The beautiful collection at Little Norway includes antiques, an ornate reproduction of a 12th century stavkirke (Norwegian timbered church) and other fascinating buildings including a stabbur and a house with a sod roof. Open spring through fall, Little Norway is twenty-five miles west of Madison, Wisconsin.

The Chapel in the Hills
Rapid City, South Dakota
This stave church duplicates one built more than eight hundred years ago in Borgund, Norway. Carved dragon heads are on the roof. There is also an imported Norwegian stabbur (a building used for storage of food).

The Nordic Heritage Museum
Seattle, Washington
This facility is devoted to the people from the five Scandinavian countries: Sweden, Norway, Finland, Denmark and Iceland.

The Heritage-Hjemkomst Center
Moorhead, Minnesota
The center features a twentieth-century Viking ship and exhibits that tell the story of the Red River Valley.

'I Jesu Navn'
Norwegian Table Prayer

I Jesu Navn går vi til bords,
Spise og drikke på ditt ord.
Deg Gud til aere, oss til gavn
Så får vi mat i Jesu navn.

In Jesus' name we take our place,
To eat and drink upon Thy grace.
To Thy honor and our gain
We take our food in Jesus' name.

Glogg

1 bottle red port
12 figs
1/2 cup candied ginger
1 stick cinnamon
1/2 cup raisins

1/2 cup hazelnuts
1/2 cup slivered almonds
2 Tbs. dried orange peel (optional)
1 cup cubed sugar

Soak all but sugar overnight in the port. Before serving, bring to a slow boil and pour over sugar. Serve warm. 1/2 pint vodka or brandy can be added if a stronger drink is desired. Serves about 15 with one refill.

Fruit Juice Glogg

2 cups apple juice	4 cloves
1 cup grape juice	1 orange peel, pared from orange
2 Tbs. sugar	1/3 cup slivered almonds
1 stick cinnamon	1/3 cup raisins

Combine juices, sugar, spices and orange peel in a saucepan. Bring to a boil. Remove cloves, cinnamon stick and orange peel. Place several almonds and raisins in punch cups and pour hot punch over them. Best to serve hot punch immediately.

Norwegian Eggcream

Eggedosis

10 egg yolks
1/2 cup sugar

1 cup brandy
nutmeg

Beat egg yolks and sugar together until thick and creamy. Gradually beat in brandy. Sprinkle with nutmeg. Makes 1 quart.

Split Pea Soup   **Ertesuppe**

1 cup split peas
1 small ham hock
2 quarts water

2 medium-sized carrots
1/2 small onion, finely chopped
salt to taste

Wash peas and soak overnight in enough water to cover. In the morning, boil the ham hock in water for 1/2 hour. Add the peas and soaking water to the ham hock kettle, cover and boil slowly until the peas are mushy, about 1 hour. Remove the ham hock. Scrape and slice carrots and add, with onion, to cooked peas. Salt if necessary. Cook for another 30 minutes. If there is meat on the ham hock, chop fine and return to soup. Serves 6.

Spinach Soup   Spinatsuppe

2 lbs. fresh spinach, chopped   1 tsp. salt
2 quarts chicken stock   1/4 tsp. white pepper
3 Tbs. butter   dash nutmeg
2 Tbs. flour   3 hard-cooked eggs, sliced

Add chopped spinach to boiling chicken stock; simmer for 8-10 minutes. Strain spinach from the broth and set aside. Melt butter in a saucepan; whisk in the flour and gradually add 1 to 2 cups of the chicken stock, stirring until well-blended. Add the flour mixture to the hot stock, stirring constantly with wire whisk; simmer over low heat for about 5 minutes. Add spinach and continue to simmer, uncovered, for 5 minutes longer. Serve with egg slices on top. Makes 4-6 servings.

Yellow Pea Soup

Gul ertesuppe

2 cups dried yellow peas
2 lbs. boneless pork shoulder
3 leeks, sliced
2 medium-sized carrots, scraped and
    shredded
2 medium-sized onions, chopped

2 tsp. chopped parsley
1 tsp. crushed marjoram
1/2 tsp. crushed thyme
1/4 tsp. ground ginger
1 tsp. salt
spicy brown mustard (optional)

Wash peas thoroughly, then heat to boiling in 7 cups cold water. Boil a few minutes, remove from heat, and let soak for 30 minutes. Add pork shoulder and rest of ingredients, except mustard, and heat to boiling. Reduce heat and simmer partially covered for about 1-1 1/2 hours, until pork and peas are tender. Remove pork from soup, cut into thin slices, and serve with mustard, if desired.

Cauliflower Soup   Blomkålsuppe

2 Tbs. vegetable oil
1/2 cup chopped onion
1 small carrot, peeled and grated
1 cup chopped celery
1 medium-sized head cauliflower, cut
      into flowerets
2 Tbs. chopped parsley
8 cups chicken stock

"bouquet garni" (1/2 tsp. peppercorns,
      1 tsp. tarragon, 1/2 bay leaf)
1/4 cup butter
1/4 cup flour
2 cups milk
1 cup half-and-half
salt
1 cup sour cream

Heat oil in large stockpot over medium heat. Sauté onion until tender. Add carrot and celery and sauté lightly. Add cauliflower and 1 Tbs. parsley; reduce heat,

15

(contd.)

cover, and cook for about 15 minutes; stir occasionally. Add chicken stock and bouquet garni and bring to a boil; reduce heat and simmer for about 5 minutes. To thicken, melt butter in saucepan; stir in flour and slowly add milk, stirring constantly until thick. Remove from heat and stir in half-and-half. Stir sauce into simmering soup. Season to taste with salt and simmer for 15-20 minutes. Before serving, remove bouquet garni; mix about 1/2 cup hot soup with sour cream. Stir sour cream mixture into soup; add remaining parsley and reheat. Makes 10-12 servings.

Tomato Soup   Tomatsuppe

4 medium-sized tomatoes   salt and pepper
pinch baking soda   butter
2 cups whole milk   Spekekjött (dried beef)

Wash, peel and slice the tomatoes. Place in a medium-sized sauce pan and cook over medium heat until very soft. Remove from heat. Add the pinch of soda to the tomatoes to prevent curdling. In another pan, bring milk to a boil and remove from heat. Force the cooked tomatoes through a strainer and add to the milk. Season to taste with salt, pepper and butter. Serve with Spekekjött (dried beef).

Cucumber Soup   # Agurksuppe

1 Tbs. butter
1/2 medium-sized onion, chopped
1 medium-sized carrot, sliced
4 cups chopped celery with leaves
3 medium-sized cucumbers, peeled
        and diced
1/4 tsp. thyme

1/2 tsp. tarragon
6 cups chicken broth
2 eggs
1 cup cream
1/8 tsp. lemon juice
sweet paprika
sesame seed

Sauté onion, carrots and celery in butter until almost tender. Add cucumbers, thyme, tarragon and chicken broth; cook, covered, until vegetables are soft. Purée and return to low heat. Beat eggs with the cream and lemon juice.

(contd.)

Gradually add about 1 cup of the hot soup to this mixture. Add egg mixture slowly to soup, stirring constantly until well-blended and creamy. Season to taste. To serve, sprinkle with sweet paprika and sesame seed.

Cheese Soup   Ostesuppe

2 cups chopped celery
1/2 large green pepper, chopped
2 cans cream of mushroom soup
milk equal to 2 cans soup
1/2 cup tomato purée
1/4 tsp. ground coriander

1/2 tsp. white pepper
2 cups shredded Cheddar cheese
1/4 cup sour cream
2 Tbs. chopped parsley
1/2 cup dry sherry (optional)

Cook celery and green pepper in boiling water until tender. Drain. Mix cream of mushroom soup and milk, then mix with celery and green pepper. Heat in a double boiler over hot (not boiling) water. Stir in tomato purée, coriander, pepper, cheese and sour cream. Stir until mixture is smooth and hot. Add sherry, if desired, just before serving. Garnish with chopped parsley.

Fish Soup

Fiskesuppe

2 Tbs. butter or margarine
4 medium-sized potatoes, diced
2 leeks or scallions, sliced
1 stalk celery, diced
2 tsp. salt

1 tsp. pepper
5 cups water
1 lb. fresh or frozen fish fillets, cut into
    1-inch pieces
1 Tbs. chopped fresh dill or 1 tsp. dried
    dill

Melt butter in large heavy stockpot; sauté potatoes, leeks and celery until glazed.
Add salt, pepper and water. Boil for about 10 minutes, until vegetables are almost
tender. Add fish and boil for 10-15 minutes longer. Sprinkle with dill just before
serving. Serves 4.

Ale Stew   Ølsuppe

1 1/2 lbs. lean beef, cut into thin slices   8 medium-sized potatoes, scrubbed
    (round steak is good)   and sliced
3 Tbs. margarine or butter   1 tsp. salt
3 medium-sized onions, sliced   1/8 tsp. pepper
                                               1 pint light ale

Brown beef slices in 2 Tbs. margarine; remove from pan and set aside. Keep warm. Sauté onions in remaining margarine until lightly browned. In a heavy saucepan, place alternate layers of meat, onions and potatoes; sprinkle with salt and pepper. Pour pan drippings over layers. Add ale, cover, and simmer gently until meat and potatoes are tender, about 1 1/2 hours. Makes 4-5 servings.

Trondheim Soup

Trondhjemssuppe

2 quarts boiling water
1/2 cup barley or rice
1/2 lb. dried pitted prunes
1/2 cup raisins
4 Tbs. fresh lemon juice

3 Tbs. sugar
1/2 cup red fruit juice (cherry or
    cranberry)
1/2 cup whipping cream
1/4 tsp. salt
2 egg yolks, beaten

Cook barley or rice in boiling water for about 1 hour. Add prunes and raisins; simmer until tender, about 1/2 hour. Combine lemon juice, sugar, fruit juice, whipping cream, salt and egg yolks; beat with a wire whisk. Add 1 cup hot stock to this mixture before blending into the soup. Add to the soup and continue to whisk until hot. May be served hot or cold.

23

Norwegian Fruit Soup

Søtsuppe

1/3 to 3/4 cup quick cooking tapioca
2 quarts water
1 can prunes, pitted
1/2 cup light and dark raisins
1 cup dried apricots
1/2 tsp. salt

2 sticks cinnamon, broken
juice of 1 lemon
1 can pitted dark Bing cherries with juice
1 cup sugar
1 pint grape juice
1 pint red wine

Soak tapioca overnight in 2 quarts water. Add prunes, raisins, dried apricots, cinnamon sticks and salt. Bring to a boil. Reduce heat to a simmer; cover and cook until tapioca is clear, stirring occasionally. Add lemon juice, cherries, sugar, grape juice and wine. Bring to a boil and remove from heat. Serve hot or cold.

Norwegian Vegetable Salad   Grønnsaksalat

1 cup finely shredded cabbage
2 carrots, peeled and grated
2 cooked beets, coarsely grated

1 apple, peeled, cored and grated
1 Tbs. lemon juice

Combine vegetables and grated apple; mix in lemon juice. Toss with *Dressing for Coleslaw (Page 30).* Serves 6.

Red Bean and Celery Salad

Salat med røde bønner og selleri

2 15-oz. cans red kidney beans
2 cups sliced celery, with leaves
6 scallions, finely sliced
DRESSING:
1/2 cup olive oil
1/2 cup red wine vinegar
2 tsp. dill seed
1 tsp. tarragon powder

1/2 medium-sized green pepper,
    coarsely chopped
1 cup chopped sweet pickle

1/2 tsp. ground cardamom
1 tsp. curry powder
1 tsp. salt

Drain and rinse kidney beans in cold water. Combine with celery, scallions, green pepper and sweet pickle. Blend all ingredients for dressing and pour over bean mixture. Marinate for at least 1/2 day.

Aquavit Herring

4 fillets of salt herring
2/3 lemon, peeled and thinly sliced
1 1/3 tsp. juniper berries, crushed

MARINADE:
5 Tbs. vinegar
1/4 cup water
1/4 cup sugar
4 whole cloves
1 slice lemon peel (1 X 2 inches)

Sild i aquavit

3/4 medium-sized onion, thinly sliced
1/3 tart apple, peeled, cored and cut
        into large julienne strips
3 Tbs. Aquavit

1/2 tsp. caraway seeds
1/2 tsp. aniseed
1/4 tsp. ground allspice
1/2 tsp. cracked black peppercorns

(contd.)

Soak herring in cold water overnight. Rinse and dry. Combine all ingredients for marinade in a saucepan and bring to a boil. Remove from heat and cool. Cut herring into 1-inch pieces and layer with lemon slices, juniper berries, onion and apple in a large glass jar or bowl. Add Aquavit to marinade and strain into layers. Cover tightly and marinate in refrigerator 1 to 2 days before serving. Can be refrigerated for 1 week.

24-Hour Salad

2 eggs, beaten
4 Tbs. sugar
4 Tbs. vinegar
2 Tbs. butter
2 cups mini-marshmallows

1 cup cream, whipped
2 cups white cherries or grapes
2 cups pineapple chunks, drained
2 oranges, sectioned or 1 small can
      mandarin oranges, drained

Combine eggs, sugar, vinegar, and butter, and cook in double boiler. Stir constantly until a thick custard is formed. Cool, then add remaining ingredients. Pour into a pretty crystal bowl and chill 24 hours.

Dressing for Coleslaw   ## Dressing til Kålsalat

1 cup white vinegar
1 tsp. celery seed
1 cup salad oil
1 cup sugar

1 tsp. dry mustard
1 tsp. salt
1 medium sized onion, grated

Heat (but do not boil) vinegar and celery seed. Set aside to cool. Combine and beat salad oil, sugar, dry mustard, salt and onion. Combine two mixtures and beat well. Shake well before using. Dressing may be kept refrigerated for 3 to 4 weeks.

30

Norwegian Rye Bread   Rugbrød

2 pkgs. dry yeast
2 cups lukewarm water
4 1/2 cups white flour
1 tsp. sugar
1 1/2 cups rye flour
2/3 cup firmly packed brown sugar
3 1/2 Tbs. dark, unsulphured molasses

3 Tbs. butter, melted
1 Tbs. finely grated orange peel
1 tsp. salt
1 tsp. vinegar
pinch aniseed
vegetable shortening

Soften yeast in 1 cup warm water. Combine 1 cup white flour and 1 tsp. sugar in a large bowl. Add yeast mixture and let stand about 5 minutes. Stir in remaining water. Add remaining white flour and all other ingredients except shortening. Stir
(contd.)

until combined. Turn onto floured surface and knead until dough is smooth and satiny, adding additional white flour if necessary. Place dough in large bowl greased with shortening; turn dough to grease all surfaces. Cover with cloth and let rise until double, about 1 hour. Punch down and return to floured surface and knead until no longer sticky. Return to bowl and coat top lightly with shortening. Cover and let rise until double, about 30 minutes. Divide dough in half and form into 2 8-inch round loaves. Place on greased baking sheets; cover and let rise until double, about 30 minutes. Bake in preheated 350° oven until lightly browned, about 25-30 minutes.

Oatmeal Flatbread

Havremel Flatbrød

1/2 cup sugar
3/4 cup melted butter
1/2 tsp. salt
1 1/2 cup buttermilk

1 tsp. soda
3 cups white flour (or 2 cups white and
   1 cup whole wheat)
2 cups quick-cooking oats

Cream together sugar and melted butter. Add salt. Add soda to buttermilk and then add to the creamed mixture alternately with flour. Add the oats. Divide mixture into 2 log shapes. Divide each into 1/3 cup portions and shape into a round ball. Press down and roll on pastry cloth with a rolling pin covered with a pastry sleeve. Roll paper-thin. Use a *lefse* stick, or roll on rolling pin.

(contd.)

Lift and unroll on cookie sheet. Either cut with pastry cutter into squares before baking or bake and then break into pieces. Bake at 350° until lightly browned, about 8 minutes. Remove, cool and stack. Store in covered container.

Butter Horn Rolls

Smørhorn

1 cake yeast
1/2 cup sugar
1 cup lukewarm milk

1/2 cup butter
salt to taste
3 eggs
4 cups flour

Crumble yeast and mix with 1 Tbs. of sugar. Combine and add lukewarm milk, remaining sugar, butter and salt. Add beaten eggs. Mix in flour to make a soft dough. Let rise until doubled. Punch down and divide into halves. Roll each half into a round, cut round into 16 pie-shaped pieces. Shape butter horn by rolling toward small end. Put in lightly greased pan to rise (not quite double). Bake at 350° until flaky, about 20 minutes. While still warm, top with butter. Makes 32 rolls.

Hardtack

2 cups white flour	1/2 tsp. salt
2 cups graham flour	1 Tbs. aniseed
1/2 cup white sugar	1/2 cup shortening
1 tsp. soda	1 1/2 cups buttermilk

Mix dry ingredients. Cut in shortening. Add buttermilk. Mix until a soft dough is formed. Roll out thin on a floured board. Cut into diamond-shaped pieces. Place on a greased cookie sheet. Bake at 400° for 12-15 minutes.

Dill Casserole Bread   Brød med Dill

1 pkg. yeast	1 Tbs. butter
1/4 cup warm water	2 tsp. dill seed
1 cup creamed cottage cheese	1 tsp. salt
2 Tbs. sugar	1/4 tsp. baking soda
1 Tbs. instant minced onion	1 egg
	2 to 2 1/4 cups flour

Dissolve yeast in warm water. Heat cottage cheese to lukewarm. Combine sugar, minced onion, butter, dill seed, salt, baking soda and egg in bowl with cottage cheese and yeast mixture. Add flour to form stiff dough. Cover and let rise until double. Punch down and turn into well-greased 1 1/2 quart casserole or 8-inch round pan. Let rise 30 to 40 minutes, or until light. Bake for 40-50 minutes at 350°. Brush with butter and sprinkle with salt.

Beer Bread   Vørterkake

2 Tbs. yeast
1 1/4 cups warm milk
5 to 6 cups unbleached flour
1/2 cup sugar
1 Tbs. salt
1/2 tsp. ground cloves

1/2 tsp. pepper
1 1/2 cups beer
1/2 cup light corn syrup
2 cups rye flour
1 cup raisins

Dissolve yeast in warm milk. Set aside for 5 minutes. Add one cup unbleached flour, sugar, salt, cloves and pepper to the yeast mixture. Cover and let stand for 40 minutes, until light and bubbly. Add the beer and syrup. Then add rye flour, raisins and enough unbleached flour to make the dough stiff. Knead about 8 to 10 minutes on floured bread board. Let rise about 1 hour. Preheat oven to 350°. Divide dough into thirds and place into 3 greased loaf pans. Let rise about 10-15 minutes. Cover with foil and bake 40 minutes.

Rusk

Kavring

1/2 cup margarine
1/3 cup sugar
1 cup white flour
1 cup whole wheat or rye flour

1 tsp. soda
2 tsp. baking powder
1/2 tsp. cream of tartar
3/4 cup buttermilk

Cream together margarine and sugar. Sift together other dry ingredients. Add to creamed mixture alternately with buttermilk. Roll flat with a rolling pin to 1/4-inch thickness on a lightly floured pastry board. Cut 2-inch rounds. Place on ungreased baking sheet and bake at 400° for 10 to 15 minutes or until lightly browned. To serve: Split each biscuit in half. Place on a baking sheet and bake at 200° about 5 minutes or until lightly browned. Makes about four dozen. Can be frozen.

Lefse

This basic recipe was developed by Ida Sacquitne, a recognized expert on making Lefse, and is in the book Notably Norwegian. *Note: Sugar is often omitted in Norway.*

5 cups riced potatoes	2 cups flour
1/2 cup margarine	1 tsp. salt
3 Tbs. powdered sugar (optional)	

Use Idaho Russet potatoes. Boil, then rice potatoes through a potato ricer. Add margarine while potatoes are still warm. Cool to room temperature. Add powdered sugar, flour and salt. Mix with your hands. Knead well and then roll into a log. Cut and measure into 1/3 cup portions and make round ball of each portion. Press it down by hand and it will be easier to keep round while rolling out.

(contd.)

Dust the large canvas-like cloth *lefse* "board" with flour. Press dough down, turn over, and press down again. With a pastry sleeve covered rolling pin, roll as thin as possible into large 14-inch circles to fit *lefse* grill. The secret of making thin *lefse* is using a covered rolling pin. For an even thinner dough, use a grooved *lefse* rolling pin for the last roll across the dough. Roll dough on a *lefse* stick. Bake on *lefse* grill or griddle. Bake a minute or two, until bubbles and brown spots appear, then turn with lefse stick. Fold each *lefse* into halves or quarters. Cool between cloths and store in plastic bags. Makes about 18. Spread with butter or sprinkle with brown or white sugar. Roll up to eat.

NOTE: *Lefse* may be made without official *lefse* utensils and cloths, but take care to follow the principles of method provided by these traditional tools.

Strawberry Nut Bread — Jordbœrkake med Nøtter

1/2 cup butter
3/4 cup sugar
1/2 tsp. vanilla
1/8 tsp. lemon extract
2 eggs
1 1/2 cups flour

1/2 tsp. salt
1/4 tsp. soda
1/3 tsp. cream of tartar
1/2 cup strawberry jam
1/2 cup sour cream
1/4 cup chopped walnuts

Cream butter, sugar, vanilla and lemon extract until light. Add eggs, one at a time beating well after each. Combine strawberry jam and sour cream and add alternately with dry ingredients to creamed mixture. Add walnuts. Bake in a greased loaf pan for 50 minutes at 350°. Cool for 10 minutes before removing from pan.

Oatmeal-Date Bread

1 cup boiling water
1 cup quick rolled oats
2 eggs, beaten
1/2 cup white sugar
1 cup brown sugar
1/2 cup shortening
1/2 cup chopped dates

Harvrekake med dadler

1/2 cup chopped nuts
1 cup flour
1/2 tsp. cinnamon
1 tsp. soda
1/2 tsp. cloves
1 tsp. salt

Combine boiling water and oats and let stand until cool. Mix eggs, brown sugar, white sugar, shortening, dates and nuts. Sift dry ingredients together and stir into date-nut mixture. Add oatmeal mixture. Bake in greased loaf pan about 1 hour at 350°.

Christmas Bread

Julekake

2 cups milk, scalded
1 to 2 cakes yeast
1/4 cup warm water and 1 Tbs. sugar
1 cup sugar
7 to 8 cups flour
1/2 cup butter

1 cup raisins
1 cup chopped citron
2 tsp. cardamom
1/2 cup blanched almonds
2 tsp. salt
2 eggs

Cool scalded milk to lukewarm. Dissolve yeast in warm water and 1 Tbs. sugar. To the milk, add 1 cup sugar, yeast mixture and half the flour. Beat well. Add butter, fruit, cardamom, almonds, salt, eggs, and remaining flour to make stiff dough. Knead, cover and let rise to double. Punch down and form two loaves. Let rise. When double, bake at 350° for about 1 hour.

Waffles

Vafler

4 eggs, separated
2 cups milk
3 cups sifted flour
5 tsp. baking powder

1 tsp. salt
2 tsp. sugar
2/3 cup melted butter or margarine

Beat egg yolks, add milk, sifted dry ingredients and melted butter. Beat egg whites and fold into yolk mixture. Pour into greased, hot waffle iron. Cook until edges are lightly browned.

Poppy Seed Bread

Valmuefrøkake

3 eggs
2 1/4 cups sugar
3 cups flour
1 1/2 cups oil
1 1/2 cups milk

4 Tbs. poppy seed (less if preferred)
1 1/2 tsp. almond extract
1 1/2 tsp. butter extract
1 1/2 tsp. baking powder
1 tsp. salt

Cream eggs and sugar and add remaining ingredients. Mix well. Divide and pour into 3 small, greased and floured loaf pans. Bake at 350° for 1 hour and spread with topping.

TOPPING:
1/2 tsp. each vanilla, butter , and almond extract

1/4 cup orange juice concentrate
3/4 cup powdered sugar

46

Apple Coffee Cake

Eplekake

1 pkg. yeast
1/2 cup warm water
4 cups flour
1 tsp. salt
6 Tbs. sugar
1 cup margarine or butter
1 egg

1 cup milk
3 cups sliced apples
cinnamon
1 stick margarine or butter
2 cups sugar
1/3 cup flour

Mix yeast and warm water; set aside. Work with fingers or pastry blender 4 cups flour, salt, 6 Tbs. sugar and 1 cup margarine, until small particles are formed. Add egg, milk and yeast mixture. Let stand overnight.

(contd.)

In the morning, divide dough and press out on 2 large cookie sheets. Pare and slice apples and layer on top of each coffee cake. Sprinkle cinnamon liberally over apples. Combine 1 stick margarine with 2 cups sugar and 1/3 cup flour. Mix with pastry blender and spread over coffee cake. Bake at 350° for 15-20 minutes.

Mother's Doughnuts

Mors Smultringer

2 eggs, beaten
1 tsp. vanilla
1 cup sugar
3 Tbs. melted shortening
1 cup milk

1/2 tsp. salt
1 tsp. almond extract
1 tsp. nutmeg
2 1/2 tsp. baking powder
3 1/4 to 3 3/4 cups flour
oil for deep frying

Mix all ingredients in order given and spoon onto a floured board. Toss lightly to coat with only enough flour to make a very soft dough, just firm enough to handle, not sticky. Pat to flatten and cut with a well-floured double cutter or two sizes of biscuit cutter. Gather cutting scrap and repeat. Heat oil gradually to about 350° and maintain medium temperature. Fry doughnuts until browned on each side, turning once. Place on absorbent paper to drain.

Potato Pancakes   Potetpannekaker

2 cups grated raw potatoes   1 tsp. salt
1/4 cup milk   1 tsp. baking powder
2 eggs, slightly beaten   1/4 cup flour

As potatoes are grated, add milk at once to keep them from discoloring. Add remaining ingredients. Drop spoonfuls on hot greased skillet and fry to golden brown on both sides. Reduce heat after they are browned and cook until potatoes are done. Good with pork sausages.

Some Sandwich Suggestions

Both open-faced and "filled" sandwiches are typical light Norwegian fare. The following is a compilation of some of our favorite sandwich combinations.

1. Smoked salmon with European scrambled eggs.
2. Liver paté with beets and olives.
3. Sliced pork roast with cold Sweet-Sour Cabbage (Surkål).
4. Crab meat with capers, mayonnaise, chives, cucumber, and lemon wedges.
5. Russian salad, radish and cucumber.
6. Roquefort on dark bread with ripe olives and radishes.
7. Meatball with sweet pickle, pimiento, olive and parsley.

8. Pork with sweet mustard, cucumber and green pepper.
9. Egg salad with curry, sweet pickle and parsley.
10. Cream cheese and pineapple.
11. Finely chopped pecans and seedless raisins blended with mayonnaise.
12. Mashed bananas, peanut butter and mayonnaise.
13. Sardines and chopped hard-cooked eggs, moistened with lemon juice and Worcestershire sauce.
14. Crab meat and minced celery, mixed with salad dressing.
15. Ground leftover pot roast with celery and pickles, moisten with mayonnaise.
16. Caviar on lettuce with sliced hard-cooked eggs or scrambled eggs.

Liver Paté

Leverpostei

1 lb. calf liver, cut into 1-inch chunks
1 1/4 lbs. pork fat, 1/2 lb. cut into
  1-inch chunks
1/2 cup chopped onion
4 anchovy fillets, chopped
2 Tbs. butter
2 Tbs. flour
1 cup heavy cream
3/4 cup milk

3 eggs
1 tsp. salt
1/2 tsp. white pepper
1/2 tsp. ground allspice
1/2 tsp. crushed marjoram
1/4 tsp. ground ginger
1/4 lb. fresh mushrooms, chopped
1/4 cup dry white wine

(contd.)

Finely grind liver and 1/2 lb. pork with onions and anchovies. Prepare white sauce: melt butter, stir in flour until blended. Whisk in cream and milk; cook over low heat until smooth and thick. Stir 1/2 cup of white sauce into ground liver mixture. Mix in remaining ingredients except rest of pork fat. Cut remaining pork fat lengthwise into 1/8-inch-wide strips. Arrange overlapping strips to cover bottom and sides of a 9 X 5-inch loaf pan, or comparable mold. Reserve enough strips to cover top of paté. Shape liver mixture into prepared pan and cover top with pork fat strips. Cover and place in pan of water and bake at 350° until knife inserted in center comes out clean, about 2 hours. Remove baking pan from water and cool to room temperature before refrigerating. Chill thoroughly. Remove from loaf pan and serve, cut in thin slices.

Salmon Sandwiches   Lakesesmørbrød

1/2 lb. fresh cooked salmon, flaked or   1/4 cup chopped ripe olives
     one 7 3/4-oz. can salmon   3 scallions, chopped
1 1/2 cups shredded Swiss cheese   1 tsp. Worcestershire sauce
1/2 cup mayonnaise   1 medium-sized loaf French bread
1/2 cup finely chopped celery   softened butter

Combine all ingredients except bread and butter. Slice bread loaf in half, lengthwise. Spread both halves with softened butter and salmon mixture. Place under broiler and heat just before serving, about 5 minutes. Cut individual pieces, open-faced, to serve.

Pressed Sandwich Meat   Rullepølse

2 1/2 lbs. beef flank
4 tsp. salt
1 Tbs. pepper
2 tsp. ginger
1/2 tsp. sugar

1 lb. beef round, thinly sliced
1/2 lb. pork tenderloin, sliced
1/4 lb. beef, finely ground
1/4 lb pork, finely ground
3 Tbs. minced onion

Trim all fat from flank. Flatten with meat pounder. Mix salt, pepper, ginger and sugar, and rub flank with part of mixture. Place sliced beef and pork on half of flank. Combine ground beef and ground pork with remaining seasonings and minced onion. Spread over beef and pork slices. Roll meat tightly; tie together with strong string and secure in piece of cheesecloth. Put in a heavy kettle and cover with water. Simmer for 2 1/2 - 3 hours, until tender. Remove from kettle.

(contd.)

Place roll between two heavy plates under heavy weight to press out moisture. Keep in a cool place several hours or overnight. Remove cloth and string. Refrigerate. Serve cold, cut in thin slices. Makes 10 to 12 servings.

Spareribs

4 lbs. pork spareribs
1/2 cup chopped onion
2 Tbs. vegetable oil
1 cup catsup
1/4 cup vinegar
2 Tbs. Worcestershire sauce

1 1/2 to 2 Tbs. sugar
1 tsp. pepper
2 tsp. chili powder
1/4 tsp. paprika
1 tsp. salt
1 cup water

Cut spareribs into 3 to 4 portions. Bake uncovered at 450° for 20 minutes. Brown onions in oil, then add all other ingredients. Simmer slowly for 20 minutes. Pour sauce over partially baked ribs and continue baking at 350° for 1 1/2 hours. Baste frequently.

Mock Beef Stroganoff

1 lb. hamburger
1/2 cup chopped onion
1 tsp. salt
1 tsp. seasoned salt
1 tsp. Worcestershire sauce

dash: celery salt, garlic and sage
1/4 cup catsup
1/4 cup flour
1 1/3 cups buttermilk
6 oz. noodles
1 can French onion rings

Brown hamburger and onion, and add remaining ingredients, except noodles and onion rings. Cook and drain noodles. Add to hamburger mixture. Bake 20 minutes at 350°. Sprinkle onion rings over top. Return to oven and bake for another 10 minutes.

Meatballs   Kjøttboller

2 quarts water
1 medium-sized onion
few stalks celery, finely chopped
mixture of ground pork, beef and veal
  (preferably unseasoned)

1 cup cream
1 egg
1 Tbs. cornstarch
salt and pepper

GRAVY:
2 cans consommé
3 Tbs. flour

1 can cream of mushroom soup

(contd.)

Bring water, onion, and celery to a boil in a deep kettle. Mix ground meat, cream, egg, cornstarch, and seasonings, and form balls. Drop meatballs into boiling liquid, reduce heat and simmer until they are firm. Remove from broth and put meatballs into a greased baking dish. Mix consommé, flour and mushroom soup, then pour over meatballs. Bake at 350°, covered, for 1 hour. Uncover and bake 1/2 hour more until well-browned. This can be prepared and frozen before baking.

Royal Pot Roast

Slottsstek

2 Tbs butter
2 Tbs. vegetable oil
4 lbs. boneless beef (round, rump or chuck)
1 cup finely chopped onion
3 Tbs. flour
1 Tbs. dark corn syrup
2 Tbs. white vinegar
2 cups beef stock

1 large bay leaf
6 anchovy fillets, washed and drained
1 tsp. whole peppercorns, crushed and tied in cheesecloth
salt
black pepper, freshly ground

(contd.)

In heavy 5 to 6 quart ovenproof pan or casserole, melt butter and oil over moderate heat. Brown meat on all sides. Remove meat from pan. Add onion to meat juices in pan and cook over moderately high heat 6 to 8 minutes, stirring occasionally until lightly browned. Remove from heat. Add flour. Stir gently to blend. Add dark syrup, vinegar and stock. Add bay leaf, anchovies and bag of peppercorns. Return meat to pan, cover and bring to a boil. Preheat oven to 350°. Place pan on shelf in lower third of oven, regulating heat so liquid barely simmers. Meat should be tender in about 3 hours. Transfer roast to heated platter. Cover to keep warm. Skim fat from meat juices, discard bay leaf and peppercorns. Add salt and pepper to taste. If flavor is lacking, boil briskly, uncovered, over high heat to concentrate. Serve gravy with the meat.

Fried Calf's Liver

2 lbs. calf's liver
1 pint water
1/4 cup vinegar
1 tsp. salt

1 egg, beaten
cracker crumbs (or flour)
2 Tbs. butter

Soak liver in water and vinegar for at least 2 hours. Remove membrane and cut liver into thin slices. Pat dry; salt and pepper; dip into beaten egg, then into cracker crumbs or flour. Fry in browned butter over medium heat until well done. Makes 4-6 servings.

Veal with Sour Cream

Kalvekjøtt i rømme

1/4 cup finely chopped onion
3 Tbs. butter
3 Tbs. vegetable oil
4 slices of veal, 3/8-inch thick and
        pounded to 1/4-inch thick

1 cup sour cream
1/2 cup shredded Gjetöst (goat cheese)
salt and pepper

Sauté onions in 1 Tbs. butter and 1 Tbs. oil in large heavy skillet over low heat until transparent. Remove onions from skillet and set aside. Add remaining butter and oil and sauté prepared veal slices until lightly browned. Remove to a platter and keep warm. Pour off all except a thin layer of fat from pan. Return onions and cook for a few minutes over high heat until slightly brown. Reduce heat and slowly add sour cream and cheese, a little at a time, stirring constantly until cheese melts and sauce is smooth. Do not boil. Season with salt and pepper. Return veal to skillet and simmer in sauce for 1-2 minutes.

Veal Fricassee   Kalvefrikassé

2 lbs. veal
water to cover veal
2 tsp. salt
1 Tbs. butter

1/2 cup flour
2 medium-sized carrots, sliced and
cooked
parsley, chopped

Cut the meat in several places. Place in boiling water to cover; add the salt. Boil slowly until bones can be removed easily. Remove the meat when tender; skim fat from broth. Drain and reserve broth. Melt butter, stir in flour until blended; add enough broth to make a gravy of medium thickness. Cook gravy to desired thickness. Cut meat into slices or small pieces and place on a serving dish; put cooked carrots over the top. Pour gravy over all and sprinkle with parsley.

Veal Loaf   Kalvekjøttbrød

3 lbs. veal, ground
3/4 lb. salt pork, ground
1 cup crushed crackers
2 eggs, beaten

1 cup boiling water
1 tsp. sugar
4 tsp. salt
2 tsp. pepper

Mix veal and salt pork together until well-blended. Add remaining ingredients; mix thoroughly. Shape into a greased loaf pan and bake at 300° for 2 hours.

Liver Loaf

2 lbs. ground liver
1/2 lb. chopped side pork
2 tsp. salt
1/2 tsp. pepper
1/4 tsp. nutmeg

1/4 tsp. ground cloves
2 eggs, beaten
3/4 cup milk
onion, chopped (as desired)
1 cup flour

Preheat oven to 400°. Mix all ingredients together and put into greased loaf pan. Place in preheated oven and reduce heat to 300°; bake for 1 hour. Serve warm or chilled.

Blood Sausage   Blodpølse

1/2 cup uncooked rice or 1 cup
   pearl barley
2 quarts pork or beef blood
   (pork is preferred)
1/2 cup sugar
dash ground cloves

1/2 tsp. ground ginger
1/2 tsp. ground allspice
1 Tbs. salt
3 to 4 cups flour
cloth bags, 4 x 10 inches
3/4 cup raisins (optional)
1 1/2 lbs. suet or fresh pork, diced

Cook rice or barley in boiling salted water until nearly done. Drain and combine
with blood and seasonings. Add enough flour to make a thin batter, just a little
thicker than pancake batter. Wet cloth bags. Pour batter into bags, adding raisins
(if desired) and diced suet or pork at intervals so it is distributed throughout.

(contd.)

Fill bags about 3/4 full to allow for expansion of the sausage. Sew or tie ends of bags tightly and place in slightly salted boiling water. Simmer 1 1/2 to 2 hours or until well-done. When ready to serve, remove from bags and slice.

Serving suggestions: While hot, top with butter and syrup. Slice cold and fry in pork drippings or butter until brown, cover with sour cream and simmer for 5 to 10 minutes.

Christmas Ham   Juleskinke

1 fresh ham (9 to 10 lbs.)   2 bottles light beer
1 cup sugar   2 bottles dark beer
3 Tbs. fine salt   3 cups coarse salt
4 Tbs. saltpeter

Rub ham with 1 Tbs. sugar, 3 Tbs. fine salt and 3 tbs. saltpeter. Leave 24 hours.
Boil beer, remaining sugar, coarse salt and 1 Tbs. saltpeter together. Cool and
pour over ham. Leave in brine for 3 weeks, turning daily. Hang to dry in an airy
place. Smoke according to smoker directions. When smoked, simmer 4 hours in
unsalted water. Cool in stock. Remove rind. Serve hot or cold. Store in stock to
keep ham juicy.

Ham Loaf

2 lbs. pork , ground
1 lb. cured ham, ground
1 egg, beaten
1 cup bread crumbs

1/2 cup milk
3 Tbs. tomato soup
1/2 tsp. paprika
1/4 tsp. salt
1 medium-sized onion, sliced

MUSTARD SAUCE:
1/2 cup tomato soup
1/2 cup sugar
1/2 cup mustard

1/2 cup vinegar
3 egg yolks, beaten

Mix all ham loaf ingredients except onion, and shape in a loaf pan. Arrange onion slices on top. Bake at 350 for 1 1/2 hours. Serve with mustard sauce.

To prepare sauce, mix all ingredients and cook in a double boiler, stirring constantly until thick.

Glazed Ham Balls

Glaserte skinkeboller

1/2 lb. ham, ground
3/4 lb. pork, ground
2/3 cup rolled oats (uncooked)
1 egg, beaten
1/2 cup milk
1/3 cup brown sugar

2 Tbs. flour
1 tsp. dry mustard
2/3 cup fruit juice (pineapple,
    apricot, or peach)
2 Tbs. vinegar
6 whole cloves

Combine ham, pork, rolled oats, egg and milk. Mix until thoroughly blended, and chill. Shape into balls and place in shallow baking pan. Bake at 300° for 1 hour. Drain excess fat. Combine remaining ingredients in sauce pan; cook until thick. Pour over ham balls and continue baking for 15 minutes. Serve in center of a baked noodle or rice ring, garnished with parsley and carrot petals as desired.

Lamb and Cabbage   Fårikål

3 to 4 lbs. lamb trimmed of fat and cut
    into 1 1/2-inch cubes
3 Tbs. butter or margarine
1/2 cup flour
3 cups chicken broth

1 large-sized onion, sliced
2 lbs. white cabbage, coarsely sliced
2 Tbs. salt (approximately)
pepper to taste

Brown lamb cubes in butter over medium heat a few at a time until evenly browned. Remove from pan and place in a large bowl. Sprinkle meat with flour and toss until well-coated; use all the flour. Pepper to taste.

(contd.)

In 6-quart ovenproof casserole, layer lamb cubes, onion slices and cabbage slices, using half the ingredients each time. Salt each layer lightly. End with a layer of cabbage. Pour fat from pan used to brown the meat. Pour chicken broth into pan and boil, scraping any browned meat particles from bottom of pan into the broth. Pour broth over layered meat, onion slices and cabbage slices. Bake at 350° for 1 1/2 hours or until meat is tender. Serves 6. Can be made ahead of time and reheated. Boiled potatoes and parsley go well with this.

Lamb Roast

Lammestek

1 Tbs. salt
1 Tbs. freshly ground pepper
1 5 lb. leg of lamb
3 onions, sliced
3 carrots, sliced

1 cup hot beef broth
1 1/2 cups hot strong coffee
1/2 cup heavy cream
1 Tbs. sugar

Preheat oven to 450°. Rub the salt and pepper into the lamb and place on a rack in a roasting pan. Surround the lamb with the onions and carrots. Roast 30 minutes, then skim off the fat. Reduce oven temperature to 350°, add the broth, coffee, cream and sugar. Basting frequently, continue roasting 40 minutes to 1 hour, depending on desired degree of doneness. Transfer lamb to a warm platter and force gravy through a sieve, or purée.

Roast Venison

Dyrestek

3 to 4 lbs. haunch of venison, deboned
3 Tbs. butter, softened
salt
freshly ground pepper
1 tsp. chopped parsley
pinch dried thyme

1 1/2 cups beef stock or bouillon
1 Tbs. butter
1 Tbs. flour
1 cup whipping cream
2 tsp. red currant jelly
1/2 oz. Gjetöst (goat cheese)

Rub meat with salt, pepper, parsley and thyme and spread with softened butter. Tie cord, if needed, to hold shape. Place on a rack in shallow roasting pan and sear in preheated 475° oven for about 20 minutes. When meat is browned, reduce heat to 375° and add beef stock to juices in pan. Roast uncovered for

(contd.)

about 1 1/4 hours; baste with pan juices frequently. When roast reaches desired degree of doneness, remove to large platter; cover to keep warm. Skim fat from pan juices. Measure remaining juices and reduce or add water to make 1 cup. In a saucepan, melt butter, stir in flour and cook over low heat until flour is browned, but not burned. Whisk the pan juices into flour mixture until smooth; next, add the whipping cream, jelly and cheese. Whisk until jelly and cheese are incorporated into a smooth sauce. Do not boil. Heat only until sauce is hot. Serve separately with the sliced venison.

Roast Goose   Stekt Gås

1 9 to 10 lb. goose
salt
2 lbs. tart apples, peeled, cored and
  chopped

1 lb. prunes, pitted, halved and soaked
6 Tbs. butter, melted in 1 cup hot water
flour

Wash goose thoroughly; pat dry. Rub salt inside and out. Prick thoroughly with sharp-tined fork (about every second square-inch). Stuff cavity with the mixture of apples and prunes. Place breast-side up on a rack in a large open broasting pan. Roast at 450° for 45 minutes. Remove from oven and drain off drippings. Sprinkle with a little more salt and dust with flour. Reduce oven to 350° and continue baking, allowing about 20 minutes per pound. When flour browns, baste often with water and butter mixture. Sprinkle lightly with flour after each basting to absorb excess fat.

Lobster   Hummer

lobster tails (1 8-oz. tail per serving)   1 tsp. fennel
1/4 lb. butter   1 tsp. salt
1 large onion, minced   1/8 tsp. cayenne pepper
2 medium-sized carrots, shredded   1/8 tsp. saffron
1/4 cup brandy   1/2 tsp. lemon juice
                                             2 cups heavy cream

Prepare lobster. If frozen, follow directions on package, but cook no longer than
10 minutes after liquid comes to a boil. When cooked, remove from boiling water
and rinse in cold water. Slice lobster meat into 1-inch pieces and set aside. Sauté
onion and carrots in butter until tender. Add the lobster and continue to sauté
until lobster is glazed (not brown). Heat brandy, pour over lobster and set aflame;
stir until flame dies. Blend in seasonings, lemon juice and cream. Stir until thick.
Serve over hot rice.   80

Baked Fish

Bakt Fisk

3 lbs. baking fish (bass, halibut,
   or any other firm fish)
salt and pepper
oregano
1/2 cup olive oil
3 firm tomatoes
3 green onions, chopped

3/4 to 1 cup chopped parsley
1 clove garlic
15 to 20 saltines, crushed
butter
2 large onions, sliced into rings
lemon slices for decorating
1 cup water

Place fish in greased baking pan and sprinkle with salt, pepper and very little oregano and oil. Place tomato slices, green onions, parsley and garlic over fish. Top with cracker crumbs, dot with butter and decorate with onion rings and lemon slices. Add water and bake for 45 minutes at 350°. Serves 6.

Baked Trout   Bakt Ørret

1 4 to 5 lb. fresh trout
4 cups coarse bread crumbs
1/2 cup melted fat (bacon,
   sausage or chicken)

1 tsp. salt
sage to taste
pinch of thyme
pinch of chervil

Clean trout, wipe dry and sprinkle with salt, inside and out. To prepare stuffing: mix all ingredients. Stuff fish and secure. Place on a rack in a baking pan and bake at 375°; allow 10 to 15 minutes per pound. Baste with pan juices. Serve with melted butter and lemon or a savory sauce.

Creamed Crab

Stuet Krabbe

1 cup crab meat
2 Tbs. butter
2 Tbs. flour
1 cup cream
3 Tbs. sherry

buttered crumbs
1 egg, beaten
paprika
salt
cayenne

Flake the crab meat, removing all bones carefully. Make a white sauce of the flour, butter and cream; add crab and sherry. Fill the buttered crab shells or small ramekins. Top with buttered crumbs and glaze with egg. Sprinkle paprika, salt and cayenne over top and brown in a hot oven.

Codfish

Klippfisk

1 lb. salt codfish
2 Tbs. butter
2 Tbs. flour
1 cup milk

1/4 tsp. salt
paprika
1 tsp. curry powder
onion juice

Soak codfish in cold water 2 hours to freshen. Melt butter, add flour mixed with salt, curry and paprika. Blend well, add milk gradually, stirring until very smooth. Bring to a boil; boil 2 minutes. Add onion juice to taste. Drain cod, rinse, and boil in unsalted water for 10 minutes. Serve with sauce.

Boiled Salmon

Kokt Laks

4 to 6 lbs. salmon, dressed
3 quarts water

1/4 cup lemon juice
3 Tbs. salt

SAUCE:
1/2 cup sour cream
1/4 tsp. salt

1/4 tsp. sugar
1/2 tsp. horseradish
parsley and lemon

Place clean salmon on large piece of cheesecloth. Tie ends of cloth. Bring water, lemon juice and salt to a boil in a large pot with a rack on the bottom. Lower salmon in carefully, so that it rests on the rack. Cover. Simmer 10-12 minutes or until flaky. Remove from pot and place on platter.

To prepare sauce: mix sour cream, salt, sugar, and horseradish. When ready to serve, remove cheesecloth from salmon, scrape off any skin. Garnish with parsley and lemon and serve with sauce.

Salmon Pie

Laksepai

2 Tbs. butter
1/4 cup flour
2 cups milk
1/4 tsp. butter flavoring

1 lb. can salmon or tuna
1/4 cup chopped pimiento
2 cups cooked peas
1 Tbs. minced onion
 biscuits

Melt butter, stir in flour until smooth. Add the milk, stirring constantly until thickened. Add butter flavoring. Gently fold into this mixture the salmon, peas, pimiento and minced onion. Pour into greased 2-quart casserole. Make round biscuits using your favorite recipe or 2 tubes of refrigerator rolls. Place biscuits on top of casserole. Bake 12-15 minutes at 350°.

Salmon Soufflé   Laksesufflé

1 cup milk
1 cup soft bread crumbs
1 Tbs. butter
1/2 tsp. salt

3 eggs, separated
1 1/2 cups drained flaked salmon
1 tsp. lemon juice

Scald milk. Add bread crumbs, butter and salt. Add slightly beaten egg yolks and cool mixture to lukewarm. Beat egg whites until stiff but not dry. Add salmon to milk-yolk mixture, then fold in beaten egg whites. Spoon into lightly oiled casserole. Place in pan of hot water and bake at 375° for 45 minutes.

Oyster Soufflé

Østers-Soufflé

10 oysters
2 eggs, separated
3 Tbs. butter

3 Tbs. flour
salt
pepper
1/2 cup cream

Remove the oysters from the shell and rinse; remove any broken shell. Put in a saucepan with water to cover. Simmer until the edges curl and the oysters are plump. Drain and cut each into 2 to 4 pieces. Melt the butter and add the flour and seasoning; blend until smooth, then add the cream and stir until very smooth. Boil 5 minutes, stirring constantly. Remove from the heat and cool. Add the beaten yolks, the oyster pieces and the stiffly beaten egg whites. Bake in buttered individual casseroles or one baking dish at 375° for 20 minutes.

Fish Mousse

Fiskemousse

1 lb. halibut or other tender fish	1 tsp. salt
3 egg whites	1/2 tsp. pepper
1 cup heavy cream or evaporated milk	cayenne, nutmeg, celery salt or a few drops onion juice

Finely chop fish. Put in a bowl that is set in ice water. With a wire whisk, beat in egg whites until frothy. Stir in cream or evaporated milk slowly. Salt, pepper and season to taste. Stir well and let stand 1 hour. Pour into 1 1/2-quart mold or several small timbale molds. Set in pan of water, 1-inch deep. Cover and bake at 350° for about 45 minutes, or until firm. May be cooked on top of stove over low heat, with water barely simmering. Turn out onto platter and serve with choice of sauce.

Shrimp and Cheese Casserole

6 slices bread, toasted and cubed
1 lb. prepared shrimp
1/2 lb. English cheese, grated
1/4 cup margarine

1/2 tsp. dry mustard
3 eggs, beaten
1 pint milk

Make in layers, Let stand at least 3 hours or overnight. Bake 1 hour at 350°, covered.

Macaroni and Salmon Loaf

1/2 7-oz. pkg. macaroni, cooked
1 cup milk
1 can salmon
2 cups bread crumbs

1 Tbs. butter
2 eggs, separated
1 Tbs. salt
creamed peas

Cook macaroni according to directions on the box. Beat the egg whites to stiff peaks. Mix all ingredients, folding in whites last. Bake in a casserole, placed in a pan of water, at 350° for 1 hour. Serve creamed peas over the loaf.

Roe Potato Cakes

Rogn og potetkaker

1 large fresh roe
5 potatoes, boiled and mashed
1 tsp. salt
1 tsp. flour

1 tsp. potato flour
1/2 tsp. pepper
1/2 tsp. ginger.
butter or margarine

Prick the roe and remove the membrane. Mash roe and stir into the finely mashed potatoes. Add the flour and potato flour, salt, pepper and ginger; blend throroughly. Form the potato-roe mixture into small round flattened cakes and fry them in butter or margarine until golden brown. Makes 4-6 servings.

Wild Rice

1 cup wild rice
1 Tbs. vinegar
1 packet dried onion

3 cups rich chicken stock
1 1/2 tsp. salt

Wash rice thoroughly. Cover with boiling water, let stand for 20 minutes. Drain. Place in casserole with tight cover. Mix salt, vinegar and dried onions with the chicken stock and add to rice. Cover. Bake 1 1/2 hours at 300°. Serves about 6, more if there are additions such as water chestnuts, green pepper or sliced almonds. For a complete supper dish, add chicken and mushrooms.

Basic Noodles

2 egg yolks	1/4 tsp. salt
1 tsp. softened lard	1/4 tsp. baking powder
2 Tbs. cream	sifted flour

Beat egg yolks, add lard, cream, salt and baking powder. Mix well and add enough sifted flour to make a soft dough that will roll out thin without being sticky. Turn onto a floured work space and roll very thin or to desired thickness. Cut wide strips, then stack and cut noodles to desired width. These may be cooked immediately, or dried and stored for later use. Sift flour over cut noodles before using. Noodles should be frozen if stored for a long time.

Norwegian Potato Balls   **Potetballer**

6 medium-sized potatoes, peeled,
    cooked and mashed
8 anchovy slices, finely chopped
1 Tbs. flour
1 Tbs. chopped parsley
1/2 tsp. salt

1/2 tsp. dry mustard
1/4 tsp. pepper
1/8 tsp. mace
1 egg yolk, beaten
1 cup dry bread crumbs
vegetable oil for deep-frying

Add minced anchovies, flour, parsley and seasonings to mashed potatoes. Shape into balls, about 1 Tbs. each. Dip potato balls into egg yolk and coat with bread crumbs. Fry a few at a time in deep fat until golden brown. Drain on absorbent paper.

Perfect Boiled Potatoes

Boiled potatoes are very popular in Norway and are served with almost every dinner. A typical Norwegian food, they are homegrown root vegetables which can be kept through the long, cold, dark winter months.

Traditional Norwegian cooks boil unpeeled potatoes, beginning with cold water, and after boiling peel and soak them in cold water for an hour. Then they recook the potatoes in salt water. When they are heated thoroughly, they are drained and returned to the pan until dry. Potatoes are kept under a cloth to absorb any excess water before serving.

Party Potatoes

8 to 10 medium-sized potatoes   garlic salt
1 8-oz. pkg. cream cheese   butter
1 cup sour cream   paprika
chives

Peel potatoes and cook until tender; drain. Mash potatoes. Beat softened cheese and sour cream until well-blended. Add to hot potatoes, beating until light and fluffy. If too stiff, thin with milk. Add chives and garlic salt to taste. Turn into a 2-quart casserole, dab with butter and sprinkle with paprika. Brown at 350° for 30 minutes. Can be made the day before, refrigerated and heated before serving.

Escalloped Potatoes

1 quart peeled, thinly sliced potatoes	2 Tbs. flour
1 1/2 tsp. salt	2 Tbs. grated onion
1/8 tsp. pepper	2 Tbs. butter
	2 cups hot milk

Place half of the potatoes in greased shallow 2-quart baking dish. Sprinkle with half the salt, pepper, flour, onion and bits of butter. Repeat and add milk. Cover and bake at 350° for 1 1/2 hours. Remove cover for last 20 minutes to brown, if desired.

Orange-Glazed Sweet Potatoes

2 lbs. sweet potatoes
2/3 cup sugar
1 Tbs. cornstarch
1 tsp. salt

1/2 tsp. orange peel, grated
1 cup orange juice
2 Tbs. butter or margarine

Heat oven to 400°. Pare sweet potatoes, cut each in half lengthwise and place in a 1 1/2-quart casserole. In small saucepan, mix sugar, cornstarch, salt and orange peel; stir in orange juice and butter and cook until thick. Pour over the sweet potatoes and bake, covered, about 1 hour, basting occasionally.

Sweet-Sour Cabbage   **Surkål**

1 head cabbage
1 tsp. salt
2 Tbs. sugar

1/4 cup vinegar
2 Tbs. caraway seeds

Shred cabbage very fine. Add other ingredients. Cover with water and simmer
for 2 to 3 hours. Good served with roast pork.

Red Cabbage   Surkål

1 large head red cabbage
2 Tbs. butter, divided
1 1/4 tsp. caraway seeds
1 Tbs. flour

1 tsp. salt
2 cups meat stock or water
1 Tbs. vinegar
1 Tbs. sugar

Cut away the core of the cabbage. Soak the head in cold salt water for 10 minutes and drain. Shred into fine strips. Grease bottom of kettle with 1 Tbs. butter, layer alternately the cabbage, caraway seed and dots of butter. Sprinkle each layer with flour and salt. Pour stock or water over all. (You should barely see cabbage.) Cover and simmer for 1 1/2 hours, stirring frequently. Do not boil dry; add a little water if necessary. Before serving, stir in vinegar and sugar. Salt to taste.

Glazed Carrots

Glaserte Gulerøtter

6 medium-sized carrots
2 cups boiling water
1 tsp. salt

4 Tbs. butter
2 tsp. sugar
1 Tbs. finely chopped parsley

Scrape and trim carrots; cut each into four pieces. Place in a saucepan and pour boiling water over them; add salt, butter and sugar. Cover with a lid, and let boil gently until the carrots are tender and water is almost evaporated. Shake the pan so that the carrots are turned and glazed. Sprinkle with chopped parsley.
Serves 6.

Baked Celery

Bakt selleri

1 large bunch celery
water to cover
1 medium-sized onion or 1 bunch
   scallions, minced
1 medium-sized green pepper,
   chopped

2 Tbs. butter
3 oz. cream cheese
3 oz. gjetöst cheese
1 1/2 cups cream
3 Tbs. dry sherry (optional)
salt and pepper

Wash and trim large bunch of celery. Cut into 1-inch pieces; include some leaves. Cook, covered in water, until almost tender. Drain and reserve liquid. Sauté onion, or scallions, and green pepper in butter until soft. Blend in 1 1/2 cups reserved celery liquid, cream cheese, gjetöst cheese, cream and sherry (if desired). Pour into lightly oiled baking dish and bake at 400° for 15 minutes, until thick. Salt and pepper to taste.

Sautéed Cucumbers   **Stekt agurk**

3 medium-sized cucumbers   1 tsp. crushed dill
6 Tbs. flour   2 Tbs. butter
1 1/2 tsp. salt   1/4 tsp. fenugreek
1/2 tsp. pepper

Pare and slice (1/4-inch thick) cucumbers. Mix flour, salt, pepper and dill; dredge cucumber slices in this mixture. Melt butter, add fenugreek. Sauté cucumber slices quickly until golden brown and crisp.

Pickled Beets

1/2 cup white vinegar
1/2 cup sugar
1-lb. can sliced beets, with juice

1/2 to 1 tsp. salt
pepper to taste
whole cloves

In a stainless steel or enameled 1 1/2- to 2-quart saucepan, combine vinegar, sugar, juice from beets, salt, and pepper. A few whole cloves tied in a cloth bag can be added, if desired. Bring mixture to a boil and boil briskly for two minutes. Place sliced beets in a deep glass, stainless steel or enamel bowl. Pour hot marinade over beets and let them cool, uncovered. When mixture reaches room temperature, cover bowl with tightly fitting cover and refrigerate at least 12 hours.

Beet Mold

Rødbetsalat i form

1 pkg. lemon gelatin
1 cup cold water
3/4 cup beet juice from canned beets
1/4 cup vinegar or lemon juice

2 cups chopped beets
2 Tbs. prepared horseradish
1/2 tsp. salt

Dissolve gelatin in cold water; add beet juice and vinegar or lemon juice. Stir in beets, horseradish and salt. Pour into ring mold, pre-rinsed in cold water. Chill until firm. Fill center with salad dressing to serve.

Berliner Kranser

3 hard-cooked egg yolks	5 cups flour
4 raw egg yolks	1 lb. butter
1 cup sugar	4 egg whites, beaten

Mash hard-cooked yolks; add sugar gradually and raw egg yolks one at a time, mixing thoroughly. Mix flour and butter until particles are finely blended. Add yolk mixture by forcing through sieve. Work by hand until it becomes a pliable dough. Roll small pieces of dough by hand to about the thickness of a pencil, about 5 inches long; lap over ends. Place in pans with waxed paper between layers and chill thoroughly. When ready to bake, dip each cookie into foamy egg white; sprinkle with sugar. Bake at 350° until golden brown, about 8 minutes. Makes about 100 cookies. Store in an air-tight container in a cool place.

Eggless Lace Cookies

Flarn uten egg

1/2 cup flour
1/2 cup sugar
1/4 tsp. baking powder
1/2 cup oats

1/3 cup butter, melted
2 Tbs. heavy cream
2 Tbs. light corn syrup
1 Tbs. vanilla

Stir together flour, sugar and baking powder; add rest of ingredients and stir well. Drop from teaspoon about 4 inches apart onto lightly oiled cookie sheet. Bake at 375° until lightly browned, about 4-6 minutes. Let stand a minute before removing to rack to cool.

Spritz

1 cup powdered sugar
1 cup butter
2 egg yolks, or 1 egg
1 tsp. vanilla

2 cups flour
1/2 tsp. cream of tartar
1/2 tsp. soda
pinch salt

Sift and tap sugar to measure 1 cup. Cream sugar and butter; add egg yolks and vanilla; mix well. Sift dry ingredients and blend into creamed mixture. Place dough in cookie press, using star tip. Shape dough into circles to form wreaths or "S" shapes. Make a test cookie; if it does not hold its shape, add a bit more flour. Bake at 350° for 6-9 minutes or until lightly browned.

Sand Bakkels

1/2 cup butter	1 tsp. vanilla
1/2 cup shortening	1/4 tsp. almond extract
3/4 cup sugar	2 1/4 cups flour
1 egg	

Cream butter and shortening with sugar; add egg and flavorings and beat well. Sift flour and gradually add to creamed mixture. Mix well. turn dough onto waxed paper and wrap. Chill for 45 minutes. Preheat oven to 350°. Cut thin slices of dough and press into sand bakkel tins, beginning at the bottom and working upward. Place on cookie sheet and bake for 15 minutes or until golden brown. Cool in tins, then turn out. (Dough may be rolled out and baked on regular cookie tins.)

Date Pinwheel Cookies

Daddelrull

1 cup brown sugar
1 cup white sugar
1 cup margarine
1 Tbs. milk
2 eggs

1 tsp. vanilla
4 cups flour
1 tsp. soda
1 tsp. salt
1 tsp. vanilla

FILLING:
1/4 cup sugar
1/4 cup water

1/4 cup nuts, finely chopped
1 pkg. pitted dates

Cookies: cream sugars and margarine. Mix in milk, eggs and vanilla. Add dry ingredients to form a firm dough. On a floured surface, roll dough to 1/4-inch thick. Mix all ingredients for filling and spread on dough. Roll up and chill for several hours. Slice and bake at 350 until golden brown, about 8 minutes.

Spiced Hermits

1 cup shortening
2 cups sugar
3 eggs
1 tsp. cinnamon
1 tsp. nutmeg
1/2 tsp. cloves

2 tsp. lemon extract
1 tsp. soda dissolved in 1 Tbs.
    hot water
2 cups raisins, rinsed and ground
3 1/2 cups all-purpose flour

Combine ingredients in order given and chill dough. Roll out thinly and cut with large round cookie cutter. Sprinkle with sugar and bake at 350° for 10 to 12 minutes. Makes a large batch.

Rosettes

2 eggs	5 drops vanilla
1 tsp. sugar	1 cup milk
1/4 tsp. salt	1 cup flour
	shortening for deep-frying

Beat eggs, sugar, salt, vanilla, milk and flour until batter is smooth. Too much beating makes rosettes blistered and tough. Have hot shortening ready in deep kettle. Leave rosette iron in hot shortening for several minutes. The iron must be hot before dipping into batter. Wipe excess fat from iron and dip hot iron in batter, being careful that batter does not come above edge of form. Place quickly in hot shortening, immerse. Fry for 20 seconds or until color desired.

(contd.)

Jolt rosette off iron and repeat. Place rosette on absorbent paper to drain. Be sure to wipe iron and reheat each time before dipping into batter. Makes 45 rosettes. When cooled, sprinkle with powdered sugar.

TIPS FOR ROSETTES:
If they do not come off the iron, they are not done enough to do so.
If blisters form, eggs have been beaten too much.
If they are not crisp, they have been fried too slowly.
If rosette falls into oil, you do not have enough flour in the batter.

Fattigmann

6 egg yolks, 3 egg whites
6 Tbs. sugar
6 Tbs. cream

2 Tbs. melted butter
6 cardamom seeds
flour
fat for frying

Beat egg yolks and whites together until thick and lemon colored. Add sugar and continue beating, add cream and beat again; blend in butter. Crush cardamom seeds to powder and add with enough flour to make a dough firm enough to roll. Roll thin as paper, cut into diamond shapes about 5 X 2 1/2 inches. Deep-fry in hot fat 2-3 minutes or until golden brown. Drain on absorbent paper and sprinkle with powdered sugar.

Hjortetakk

4 eggs, beaten
1 cup sugar
3/4 cup melted butter
grated peel of 1 orange and 1 lemon

1 tsp. baking powder
4 cups flour
4 oz. brandy

Mix all the ingredients the day before, to make dough. Refrigerate overnight. Roll small pieces of dough by hand into strips a bit thicker than a pencil and about 5 inches long. Overlap the ends of each and fry in deep fat as you would dough-nuts until browned.

Wafer Cones or Crumb Cake

Krumkake

3 eggs, well-beaten
1/2 cup sugar
1/2 cup butter, melted

1/4 tsp. salt
1/2 tsp. almond extract
1/2 tsp. lemon extract
1/2 cup flour

Mix eggs, sugar, melted butter, salt and flavoring. Beat well. Stir in flour. Heat *Krumkake iron* on medium heat. Pour a teaspoon of batter on iron, bake about one minute, turn iron over and bake until very lightly browned. Remove from iron and quickly roll onto a cone-shoped form. Cool and store in an air-tight container.

Raspberry Cake   ## Bringebœrkake

1 1/2 cups flour   1/2 cup butter
1/2 cup sugar   1 egg
1 tsp. baking powder   1/2 jar raspberry jam, divided in half

FILLING:
1/2 cup butter   2 eggs
2/3 cup sugar   1 cup finely ground blanched almonds
1/2 tsp. almond extract   (ground like coarse meal)

FROSTING:
1/2 cup powdered sugar   2 tsp. lemon juice

(contd.)

Blend flour, sugar and baking powder. Add butter and mix, working with pastry blender or fingers. Add egg and blend with a fork until flour is moistened. Press dough evenly on bottom of a greased 9-inch by 1 1/2-inch springform pan. Spread 1/4 cup raspberry jam over dough. Cover and chill while making the filling.

For filling: Cream butter and sugar. Add extract. Add eggs one at a time, beating well, then mix in ground almonds. Spoon filling on top of jam. Bake at 350° for 50 minutes. Cool in pan and remove cake carefully. Spread remaining 1/4 cup jam over top.

Mix powdered sugar and lemon juice together and drizzle on top of jam. Can be made ahead and frozen.

Wedding Cake   Kransekake

Although this recipe appears simple, you might want to bake a few practice rings before you attempt the real thing. These portions are for 18 concentric ring mold pans (found at Scandinavian specialty shops).

1 lb. almond paste
1 lb. powdered sugar, sifted

2 egg whites, unbeaten
1/2 cup powdered sugar for kneading

In a large bowl, mix almond paste and powdered sugar. Add egg whites. Mix well. Place bowl in hot water and knead dough until it is lukewarm. Turn out on board sprinkled with 1/4 cup powdered sugar. Let rest 10 minutes. Knead 2-3 minutes. Press dough through cookie press into greased ring forms. Bake at 300° for 20 minutes. Do not remove rings from forms until thoroughly cooled. Frost each ring and place on top of one another in a conical shape to form a tree with a hollow center.

(contd.)

FROSTING:

1 1/2 cups powdered sugar, sifted   1 tsp. vinegar
1 egg white, beaten

Blend powdered sugar, egg white, and vinegar. Drizzle over cake rings, as you stack. This cake freezes very well. You may want to stack the ring sections for easier storage and use additional frosting for final assembly.

NOTE--If not using concentric baking pans: With lightly floured hands, roll small amounts of dough into a 1/2-inch-thick strip, long enough to form width of base. Make each one shorter. Dip ends into egg white and join. Place rings on lightly floured baking sheets.

Almond Cake   Fyrstekake

1 1/2 cups flour   1/2 cup sugar
1 tsp. baking powder   1/2 cup plus 1 Tbs. butter
                                          1 egg or 2 egg yolks

ALMOND FILLING:
1 cup ground almonds   2 egg whites, slightly beaten
1 cup powdered sugar

Mix dry ingredients in mixing bowl. Blend in butter with a pastry blender or with
fingertips until mixture resembles coarse flour. Beat in egg or egg yolks. Chill.
Prepare filling: Grind almonds once, then grind a second time with powdered
sugar. Blend thoroughly with beaten egg whites until mixture is firm and smooth.
Chill.

(contd.)

Press 2/3 of the chilled dough into a 6-inch round ungreased cake pan, covering sides and bottom. Spread almond mixture evenly over dough. Roll remainder of dough to 1/8-inch thickness and cut into 8 strips, 1/2-inch wide. Lay four of the strips parallel to each other across the top of the filling. Arrange remaining 4 strips at right angles, weaving to form a lattice pattern. Cut another 1/2-inch-wide strip and press around edge of cake. Bake at 375° for 25-30 minutes, or until golden brown. NOTE: If you prefer blanched almonds, scald them; unblanched give a better flavor. Cool cake on rack a few minutes before carefully loosening sides and removing from pan. Cut into wedges.

Almond Apple Cake

Mandel-Eplekake

2 cups apple slices (fresh or canned)
3 eggs

1/2 cup sugar
2/3 cup ground blanched almonds

If fresh apples are used, slice and boil with 1/4 cup water and additional 1/2 cup sugar for 5 minutes. Drain and spread evenly in buttered baking dish. Beat eggs and sugar until whites are fluffy. Fold in almonds. Pour egg mixture over the apples. Bake at 350° for 30-40 minutes. Serve cold with cream or vanilla sauce. Serves 6.

King Haakon Cake

Kong Haakon Kake

1 cup shortening
1 1/2 cups sugar
3 eggs, beaten
1 cup sour milk
2 Tbs. molasses
1 cup chopped dates

3 cups flour
1 tsp. each nutmeg and salt
1 tsp. soda
1 tsp. baking powder
1 tsp. cinnamon
1 cup chopped nuts

Cream shortening, sugar and eggs well; stir in sour milk, molasses and dates. Mix dry ingredients and add to creamed mixture. Pour into greased and floured 9x13-inch pan, bake at 350° for 40-45 minutes.

Chocolate Cake   Sjokoladekake

3 egg whites
3/4 cup sugar
1/2 cup shortening
1/4 tsp. salt
1 cup sugar
1 tsp. vanilla

1/2 cup cocoa
1/3 cup hot water
1 cup cold water
2 1/2 cups sifted flour
1 1/3 tsp. soda
1/4 cup warm water

Beat egg whites and 3/4 cup sugar until fluffy and set aside. Cream shortening, salt, 1 cup sugar and vanilla. Set aside. Make a paste of cocoa and hot water and add to cream mixture; stir until lightly blended. Add cold water and flour alternately to cream mixture. Fold in egg white mixture. Add soda dissolved in warm water and fold in gently with a wire whisk. Pour into a lightly greased 9x13-inch cake pan, and bake 35-40 minutes at 350°.

Mock Whipped Cream Frosting

1 egg
1 cup milk
1/2 cup sugar
2 Tbs. cornstarch

1/4 tsp. salt
1 tsp. vanilla
1/2 cup shortening
2 Tbs. butter
5 heaping Tbs. powdered sugar

In a double boiler, beat the egg, milk, sugar, cornstarch and salt. Cook over water until thick, add vanilla, and cool. Cover until set but not hard. Beat together shortening, butter and powdered sugar. Add to cooked egg mixture, and beat until smooth. Good on chocolate cake.

Cloudberry Cream Pie

Multekrem pai

PASTRY:
1/3 cup butter or margarine
2 1/2 Tbs. sugar
1/3 tsp. salt

1 egg yolk
1 cup flour
1/3 cup finely chopped almonds

FILLING:
2 cups cloudberries, fresh or frozen
2 egg whites
1 cup sugar
1 Tbs. lemon juice

1/4 tsp. vanilla
1/4 tsp. almond extract
1/4 tsp. salt
1 cup whipping cream

(contd.)

Pastry: Preheat oven to 400°. Grease 10-inch pie pan. Cream butter, sugar and salt; add egg yolk and beat well. Stir in almonds and flour. Press into pan and bake about 12 minutes, until lightly browned. Let cool.

Filling: Mix all ingredients except cream, and heat until mixture thickens, about 15 minutes. Cool. Whip cream and fold into cooled cloudberry mixture. Spoon into pastry and freeze for at least 8 hours. Serves 12.

Caramel Pudding

Karamellpudding

2 cups sugar
3 Tbs. boiling water
3 egg yolks
2 Tbs. sugar
1 cup milk

1 tsp. vanilla
1/2 cup heavy cream, whipped
chopped walnuts (optional)
3 cups puréed fruit (applesauce or
berries)

Melt 2 cups sugar over low heat in heavy saucepan; stir until golden brown. Add boiling water slowly to melted sugar; stir until well-blended. In top of double boiler, combine egg yolks and additional 2 Tbs. sugar, milk and vanilla. Beat with wire whisk until foamy; cook until hot. Add melted sugar (should be cooled to a "soft ball") to custard. Continue beating until mixture is smooth. Remove from heat and beat until cool. Fold whipped cream into cooled custard. Sprinkle with chopped nuts, if desired. Chill and serve over fruit.

Caramel Ice   Karamell-is

1 quart whipped cream   2/3 cup coarsely ground scalded
2/3 cup sugar   almonds
1/4 cup strong boiled coffee

Stir sugar in a heavy skillet over low heat until browned. Add coffee and almonds; stir until blended. Cool and fold into whipped cream. Chill thoroughly or freeze. Makes 6 servings.

Macaroni Pudding

1/2 lb. uncooked macaroni
1 1/2 quarts milk
1 Tbs. sugar

1 Tbs. butter
4 egg yolks
4 egg whites, stiffly beaten

Cook macaroni in milk until tender. Remove from heat; add sugar and butter, mix thoroughly and let cool. Stir in egg yolks, one at a time; then fold in stiffly beaten egg whites. Spoon into a greased and floured mold which is placed in a pan of boiling water. Bake at 300° for 1 hour. Let cool slightly before removing from mold. Unmold on a platter and serve with your choice of sauce.

Bread Pudding

Brødpudding

4 cups stale cubed bread	1/2 cup sugar
2 eggs or 4 egg yolks	1 tsp. nutmeg
2 cups milk	raisins (optional)

Spread bread cubes in a lightly greased baking dish. Beat eggs, milk, sugar and nutmeg, pour over bread and let stand about 1 hour. Add raisins (if desired) and bake 30 minutes at 350°. Serve with cream, jelly or pudding sauce.

VARIATIONS:
Fruit and nuts—Add 1 cup chopped dates, raisins or figs, 1/2 cup nut meats.
Butterscotch—Instead of white sugar, use brown sugar and heat it with butter.

Dravle

2 quarts milk
2 eggs
1 quart buttermilk

1 1/2 cups sugar
1 1/2 cups raisins

Heat milk until it comes to a boil. Beat eggs into buttermilk. Add to hot milk slowly, to form cheese curds and whey. When cheese settles, reduce heat and simmer for 15-20 minutes. Add sugar and raisins. Increase heat and cook 1/2 hour or longer. Thicken with cornstarch mixed with cream, if necessary.

Rommegröt

| 1 quart cream (not too fresh) | 3/4 quart milk |
| 1 cup flour (more if needed) | sugar and salt to taste |

Stirring constantly, bring cream to a full boil and boil until foam is gone. Add flour gradually, to make a thick mush. Stir until butter appears. Remove butter and reserve. Bring milk to a boil. Add hot milk gradually to mush, stirring constantly. Simmer 10 to 20 minutes, stirring frequently until mixture thickens. Add sugar and salt to taste. Serving suggestions: Top with reserved butter; serve with syrup or honey, garnish with cinnamon and sugar.

Lemon Custard   Sitronkrem

2 Tbs. butter   few grains salt
1 cup sugar   5 Tbs. lemon juice
3 eggs, separated   rind of 1 lemon, grated
4 Tbs. flour   1 1/2 cups milk

Cream butter, sugar and egg yolks. Add flour, salt, lemon juice, and rind, then milk. Beat egg whites to stiff peaks. Fold into mixture. Spoon into greased custard cups. Place in pan of water and bake 45 minutes at 350°. Each cup will contain custard at the bottom and sponge cake at the top. Serves 8.

Rice Pudding

Risengryn Pudding

4 eggs, slightly beaten
1/2 cup sugar
dash salt
1 tsp. vanilla

4 cups milk, scalded
3/4 cup uncooked rice
1 to 1 1/2 cups raisins (optional)

Mix eggs, sugar, salt and vanilla. Add scalded milk. Add rice, and raisins, if desired. Pour into a flat baking dish. Set in another pan of water and bake at 350° for 20 minutes, stir and continue baking for 25 minutes.

Apple Dumplings with Cinnamon Sauce

Epler i slåbrok med kanel saus

1 1/4 cups sifted flour
3/4 tsp. salt
3/4 cup shortening
7 to 8 Tbs. ice water

6 tart apples, cored and pared
1/2 cup sugar
1 1/2 tsp. cinnamon
1 Tbs. butter

CINNAMON SAUCE:
1 cup sugar
1/4 tsp.cinnamon

4 Tbs. butter
2 cups water

Sift flour and salt together. Cut in shortening to a fine "meal" with some pea-sized particles. Sprinkle ice water over mixture and blend with fork. Roll out 1/8-inch thick on lightly floured board. (Dough may be divided for easier handling.)

(contd.)

Cut into six 7-inch squares. Place each apple on a square of pastry, fill each center with cinnamon and sugar. Dot with butter. Moisten points of pastry with water, bring opposite points up over apples, and seal well. Place 2 inches apart in baking pan and chill thoroughly.

Prepare sauce: mix all ingredients in a saucepan, boil 3 minutes. Pour hot sauce over chilled dumplings and bake 5-7 minutes at 500°. Serve dumplings with hot syrup and cream, if desired.

Tips for Making Sauces:

1. Never use high heat.

2. Remove sauces-in-progress from heat before stirring in fresh ingredients.

3. If additions to hot sauce are cold, adjust them by mixing in a separate container with small amount of the hot liquid before adding to the cooking pot. (This is especially important for egg or cream based sauces.)

Onion Sauce   Løksaus

3 Tbs. butter or margarine
2 medium-sized onions, finely chopped
2 Tbs. flour
1/2 tsp. salt

1/4 tsp. black pepper
1/2 tsp. sugar
1 1/2 cups milk
2 Tbs. chopped green pepper (optional)

Sauté onions in butter or margarine over medium heat, until tender. Remove onions from skillet. Stir flour, salt, pepper and sugar in remaining butter or margarine. Continue stirring over low heat and gradually add milk. Cook and stir until sauce thickens. Stir in onions and cook until blended. Stir in green pepper, if desired. This goes well with fried fish.

Egg Sauce

Eggesaus

1/4 lb. butter
1/4 cup hot stock
2 hard-cooked eggs, finely chopped
1 Tbs. finely chopped parsley

1 medium-sized tomato, peeled,
    seeded and chopped
1 Tbs. finely chopped chives
salt and pepper

Melt butter in a saucepan. Remove from heat and beat in hot stock. Stir in eggs, tomato, parsley and chives; salt and pepper to taste. Reheat to almost boiling, but do not cook. Serve immediately. Very good with poached or baked cod.

Horseradish Sauce

Pepperrot saus

4 Tbs. grated horseradish root (or
      prepared horseradish)
1 pint sour cream
1 tsp. salt

1/8 tsp. white pepper
2 Tbs. finely chopped onion
1 tsp. vinegar
3 Tbs. finely chopped dill

Drain liquid from horseradish. Combine remaining ingredients. Mix together until smooth. Makes 2 cups of sauce.

Shrimp Sauce   **Rekesaus**

2 Tbs. butter   paprika
2 Tbs. flour   1 egg yolk
1 cup boiling water   1 cup shrimp meat or 1 8-oz. can shrimp
juice of 1/2 lemon   1 Tbs. butter
salt

Melt, but do not brown, the butter. Blend in the flour, and gradually add the
boiling water, stirring constantly until the mixture thickens and is very smooth.
Add salt, paprika and lemon juice. Remove from the heat and add the slightly
beaten egg yolk and shrimp (if using lobster, omit egg yolk from recipe), cleaned
and broken into small pieces. Add the tablespoon of butter in bits just before
serving. (You can use lobster meat for lobster sauce if desired. If using lobster
omit one egg yolk.)   144

Curry Sauce

Karrisaus

2 Tbs. butter
2 Tbs. flour
2 tsp. curry powder
1/4 tsp. salt

paprika
1 cup milk
onion juice

Melt the butter; blend in the flour mixed with curry, salt and paprika. Add milk gradually, stirring until the sauce boils. Boil several minutes, stirring all the time. Add onion juice to taste.

Mock Hollandaise Sauce

Falsk Hollandais saus

2 egg yolks (slightly beaten)
1/4 cup cream
1/2 tsp. salt

1/8 tsp. nutmeg
1/2 lemon
2 Tbs. butter

Beat the yolks and cream together with a fork. Add other ingredients, except butter, and cook in double boiler until thick, stirring all the time. Add 2 Tbs. butter slowly. Serve at once.

Caper Sauce   Kaperssaus

2 Tbs. Butter   pepper
1 heaping Tbs. four   1/2 tsp. lemon juice
1 cup boiling water or fish stock   2 Tbs. drained capers
salt   1 Tbs. butter

Melt 2 Tbs. butter. Blend in flour. Add stock or boiling water gradually. Stir until
very smooth and cook until thick. Stir well. Add the seasonings, lemon juice and
capers. Add 1 Tbs. butter in small pieces. Serve immediately.

Anchovy Sauce

Ansjossaus

1/2 tsp. chopped onion
3 Tbs. butter
3 Tbs. flour
1 cup soup stock

1/3 tsp. pepper
1 tsp. lemon juice
2 anchovies or prepared paste

Brown the onion in the butter. Remove the onion. Brown the butter. Add the flour and brown with the butter. Add stock, stirring until smooth. Season with pepper and bring to a boil. Boil for two minutes, stirring constantly. Add the anchovies, cleaned and chopped fine, or anchovy paste to taste. Stir in the lemon juice. Taste and add salt if necessary. Anchovies are very salty and you may not need any more salt.

Tomato Butter

Tomatsmør

8 Tbs. unsalted butter
2 Tbs. tomato paste

1/2 tsp. salt
1/4 tsp. sugar

Beat the butter until light and fluffy, then beat in tomato paste, salt and sugar.
Chill. Serve with hot grilled or fried fish.

Cucumber Sauce   Agurksaus

1 cucumber   1/2 tsp. salt
1/2 cup heavy cream (sweet or slightly   cayenne
       sour)   2 Tbs. vinegar

Pare, chop and drain the cucumber. Chill all the ingredients thoroughly in the refrigerator. Whip the cream and mix well with the other ingredients. Serve at once. Very good on cold, boiled fish.

Whipped Cream Sauce   Fløtesaus

1 egg, separated   1/2 tsp. vanilla
2 Tbs. powdered sugar   1/2 cup cream

Beat egg yolk; add powdered sugar and vanilla. Whip cream until stiff; whip egg white until stiff but not dry. Fold cream into yolk mixture, then add beaten egg white. Fold until blended, but do not stir after peaks are formed.

Rum Egg Sauce

5 egg yolks
2 egg whites

5 Tbs. sugar
1 Tbs. rum (or brandy)

Whip egg yolks and whites together; add sugar and beat until mixture has a custard-like consistency. Beat in rum or brandy. Serve with or over fresh fruits.

Notes

BOOKS BY MAIL Stocking Stuffers POSTPAID You may mix titles. One book for $8.95; two for $16; three for $23; four for $28; twelve for $75. Please send $2.50 for a complete catalog. *(Prices subject to change.)* Please call 1-800-728-9998

American Gothic Cookbook
Cherished Czech Recipes
Dandy Dutch Recipes
Dear Danish Recipes
Fine Finnish Foods
Great German Recipes
Intriguing Italian Recipes
Norwegian Recipes **This book**
Pleasing Polish Recipes
Quality Czech Mushroom Recipes
Quality Dumpling Recipes
Recipes from Ireland
Savory Scottish Recipes
Scandinavian Holiday Recipes
Scandinavian Smorgasbord Recipes

Scandinavian Style Fish and Seafood Recipes
Scandinavian Sweet Treats
Slavic Specialties
Splendid Swedish Recipes
Ukrainian Recipes
License to Cook Arizona Style
License to Cook Iowa Style
License to Cook Kansas Style
License to Cook Minnesota Style
License to Cook New Mexico Style
License to Cook Texas Style
License to Cook Wisconsin Style
Outstanding Oregon Recipes
Waffles, Flapjacks, Pancakes (Scandinavia & Around the World.)

PENFIELD PRESS • 215 BROWN STREET • IOWA CITY, IA 52245-5842